Psyche of the Common Man

Attention Authors

Manas Publications is fighting a war to tell the world that India can win the battle not only by bullet but also by pen. We are converting fighters into writers since our country is full of intellectuals but their knowledge is only confined to them. No sincere effort has been made by any publisher to give the right direction to their knowledge and the talent of intellectual is still hidden. An author always gives the raw material in the shape of manuscript and it is the sense of publisher to make it a finished product. We are motivating the intellectuals' mind and publishing their manuscripts for more than two decades and would like to publish your manuscript too. If you or your colleagues have any manuscript or are working on, please don't hesitate to contact us with detailed synopsis and contents for its publication. We take utmost care in production and give a wide publicity to the book and its author. We can also suggest you the title for writing related to your subject, since we are the publishers who believe more in quality than in quantity.

Psyche of the Common Man

Vijay Singal, IRS
Commissioner of Income Tax

Manas Publications
New Delhi - 110 002 (India)

MANAS PUBLICATIONS
(Publishers, Distributors, Importers & Exporters)
4858, Prahlad Street,
24, Ansari Road, Darya Ganj,
New Delhi - 110 002 (INDIA)
Ph.: 23260783, 23265523 (O)
Fax: 011- 23272766
E-mail: manaspublications@vsnl.com
www.manaspublications.com

Paper Back Edition 2007

ISBN 81-7049-325-0
Rs. 165/-

Typeset at
Manas Publications

Printed in India at
Nav Prabhat Printing Press
and Published by Mrs. Suman Lata for
Manas Publications, 4858, Prahlad Street
24, Ansari Road, Daryaganj
New Delhi 110002 (INDIA)

Dedication

Dedicated in the service of Him,
who is Himself the Creator as well as
creation, at the same time.

Introduction

This book consists of some mottos, slogans and statements on various topics related to human behaviour. These thoughts have not been inspired by any specific work of the past. These proverbs rather represent the summary of the lessons learnt from day-to-day experiences. In other words, through this book, an effort has been made to give expression to common knowledge and common sense.

The intention is not to preach or to deliver sermons. Theoretically speaking, everyone knows it all. Everyone knows what is good for him and what is not. Still, a right message delivered at the right time can be of a great help. An inspirational thought can clear the confusion at the most difficult of times and show the correct path.

Since the topics covered are varied, they have been arranged alphabetically. All the thoughts under one head have been grouped together.

Contents

A

Action

An action can be termed right only
if it seems right to the individual concerned,
is approved by the society, and
does not disturb the balances established by nature.

Addiction

Addiction consists in making oneself
a slave to an object beyond one's control.
What that object is, is of little relevance.
What matters is that one has mortgaged
one's freedom to it. It is a very bad bargain.

Anger

Anger is worse than any dictator.
Till it reigns, it denies you
even the most fundamental right.
The right, that is, to think.

****

Anger is often a manifestation of
frustration and dissatisfaction with oneself,
rather than the result of
unacceptable behaviour of others.

****

Strength starves anger, while weakness fuels it.

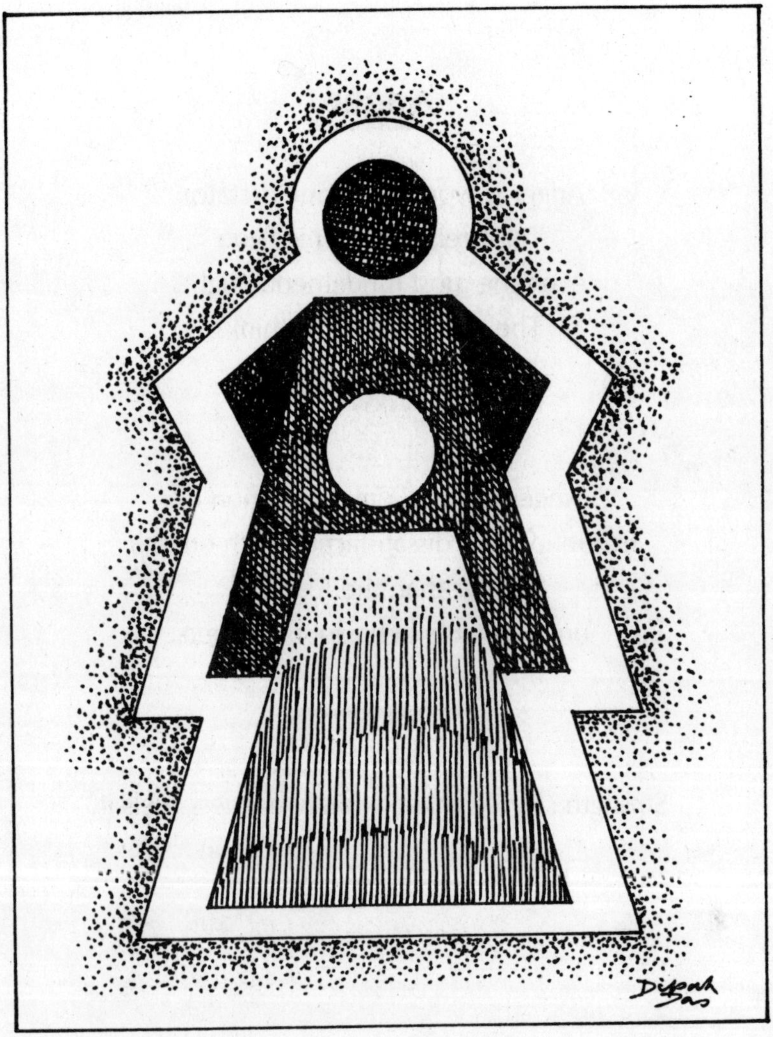

Appreciation

Words of appreciation cost nothing. But have a tremendous capacity to get things done.

Arrogance

Every successful person must have some arrogance.
Otherwise there would be no difference
between him and Him.

****

Interaction between two arrogant persons
is bound to lead to animosity.
Interaction between an arrogant and
a normal person has no meaning,
as it would be a one way traffic.
Only interaction between two normal persons
has the potential of developing into an enduring,
reasonable and purposeful relationship.

****

It is better to be proud of one's ignorance,
than to be arrogant about one's knowledge.

****

Arrogance of knowledge leads to rigidity.
Rigidity stunts growth and eventually leads to decay.

Attention

Your personal attention and genuine concern is the most precious gift you can ever give to anyone.

Attitude

One generally feels miserable because
the world does not behave as one wants.
To get over this feeling, one would have to
either change the world, or change one's liking
to bring it in tune with the world.
Choice lies with the individual concerned.

****

When you do not have control over
your own behaviour, why grumble
about the behaviour of others.

****

Human beings can be fundamentally divided into two categories, those who are generally satisfied with themselves, their surroundings and the world at large; and those who are dissatisfied with everything always. All other divisions based on sex, religion, nationality or financial status etc. are only superficial, almost redundant.

****

Happiness and contentment are the innate qualities of a man. They come from within, like the fragrance of a flower.

Awareness

Both physical strength and mental agility are important.
But only awareness enables one to relate to
these qualities as one's own.

****

Good food, physical work
and natural environment
bestow good health.
How, when, why, where and who,
are the instruments of intellect.
And awareness is the liberator of soul.

B

Behaviour

Everyone carries an inherent energy around him. Whether he converts that energy into a force of attraction or a force of repulsion depends upon his day-to-day behaviour.

Blessings

Count not your blessings for they are countless. Just thank Him for his benevolence.

C

Circumstances

Only those who can see through and look beyond the present circumstances can ever hope to change them, for the better.

Cleanliness

Cleanliness is said to be next only to godliness. Let, at least, the penultimate be achieved.

Comfort

Excess comfort generally leads to under-performance as human mind and body, over the ages, have evolved in such a manner that they excel only when faced with a challenge.

Competition

Co-operation without an inherent element of competition is nothing but total inaction; similarly, competition without an inherent element of co-operation is total annihilation.

****

Healthy competition brings out the best in you, but conflict kills all that is good.

****

When competition crosses manageable limits,
it degenerates into conflict.

****

Co-operation and competition
do not exclude each other.
In fact they are complementary,
and given the proper environment,
lead to progress and prosperity.

Compassion

An element of compassion
built into any relationship,
changes the very nature
of that relationship.

Conversion

Religions should converge; then they need not
seek to convert people or the places.

Creation

An organic entity when seen
through the clear mirror of consciousness
is found to be nothing but
happiness, peace, strength and kindness.
But, when looked at through the prism of creation,
it appears as a mind-body complex
forever struggling to find some momentary satisfaction.
The need is to understand both and draw a balance.

****

Creation is to consciousness
as statue is to clay,
as form is to substance,
and as temporary is to permanent.

****

Consciousness, which is the underlying reality behind
all creation, admits of no differentiation,
as it is an indivisible whole.
On the other hand, any two entities,
in the apparent world of creation,
have very few things in common.
When one starts minimising one's
differences with others,
one automatically starts moving from the
apparent to the real.

D

Death

Very few deaths are normal.
A great majority of them are self-induced
through uncalled for tensions and/ or unhealthy addictions.

Dedication

A life of poverty is a life of deprivation.
A life of riches is a life of depression.
Blessed are those who lead a life of dedication.

Democracy

Only those nations whose citizenry can willingly subordinate their personal interests to the collective will can hope to sustain democratic institutions, for long.

Desire

Desire is to the mind, what hunger is to the body.
If there is no desire, there can be no progress,
for there would be no economic activity.
If there is desire, there is possibility of pain,
because all desires cannot be fulfilled.
Art of living lies in striking a balance
between the two, from time to time.

Dialogue

Dialogue-less-ness is the termite that can destroy
from within even the sweetest of relationships.
From outside they seem to be normal,
from inside, they are no more.
There can be a situation of dialogue-less-ness even while
talking 24x7 if the contentious
issues are intentionally avoided.

Doubt

Doubt not your own capability.
Doubt not the sincerity of your friend.
Doubt not the fidelity of your spouse.
Doubt not the benevolence of the Lord.
Unfounded doubt only lays the foundation
of one's own destruction.

E

Education

It is the right of every individual
not only to acquire the known knowledge,
but also to explore the unknown.
The society is duty bound to play the role of a facilitator.
This is what education is all about.

****

Education is not only about
imparting the knowledge,
it must also ensure inculcation
of the right value system.

Ego

An inflated ego cannot
be fair, impartial and reasonable.
Whoever and whatever appeases it
is considered good and right.
All others and everything else
is bad and wrong.

****

Mega ego
suffers mega miseries.

End Vs. Means

Sanctity of means is as non-violable as that of the goal itself. But still, goal is the end whereas the means are just instruments utilised in achieving that goal. One's discretion has to be used judiciously, within the parameters of above statements.

Enmity

One does not remember a friend as much as one remembers a person who is perceived to be an enemy. Forgetfulness, after all, is not that bad a quality.

Environment

A specie which is, directly or indirectly, held responsible for the elimination of thousands of other species and also for the dirt, depletion and destruction of the natural resources can never hope to live in peace, ever after. If the mankind has to achieve sustainable satisfaction levels, it would have to learn to respect the sanctity of environment.

****

The Nature is an over-indulgent mother.
Let the mankind not behave as a spoilt child.

Envy

I feel envious only of those, who do not envy anyone.

Excuses

Excuses and explanations are superfluous. A success needs no explanation whereas no excuse can explain a failure.

****

Anything can be excused, but for an excuse.

F

Failure

Do not get disheartened by failure,
for there always is a next time,
provided you do not commit
the same mistake again.

Faith

In extreme grief, when all words of consolation become meaningless, it is only faith one can fall back on. Deeper the faith, greater the capacity to bear grief.

Family

Family is an umbrella that protects one from uncertainties of life; stronger the bond, better the protection.

Fate

No one can write anyone else's fate;
if one can make one's own,
that is good enough an achievement.

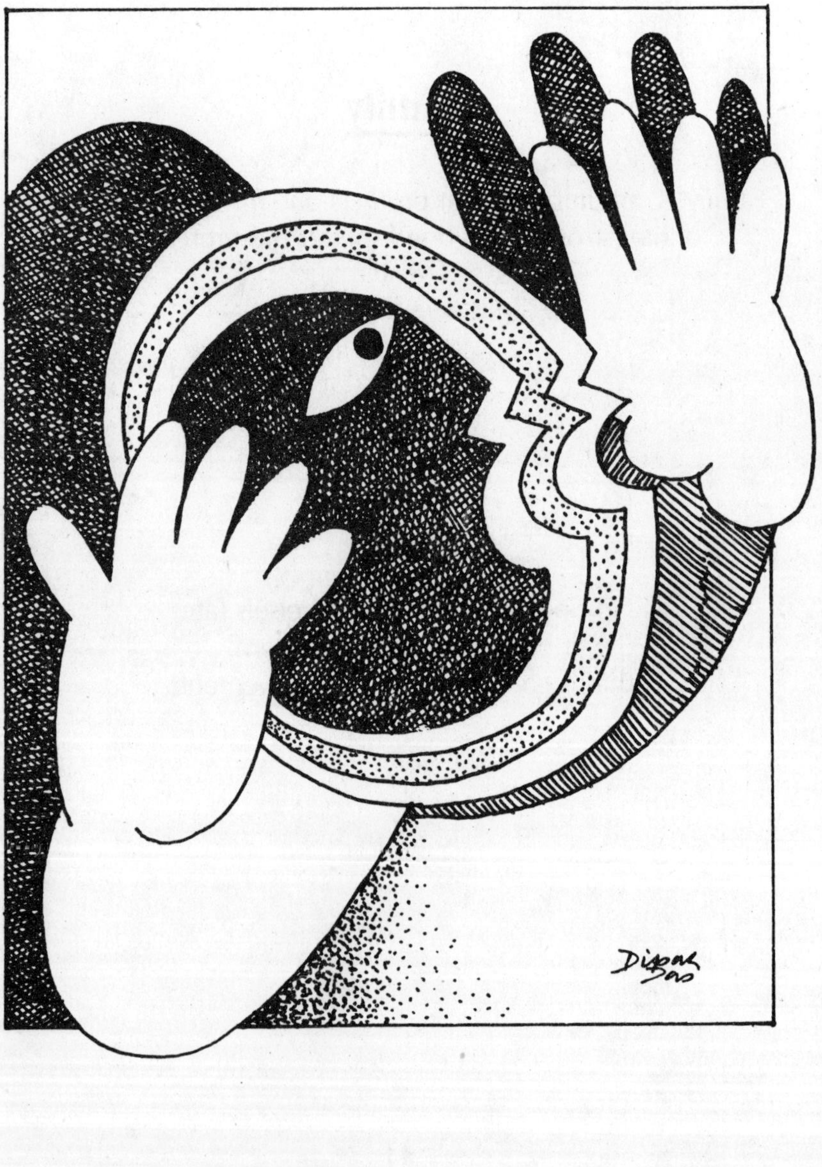

Fear

From Stone Age to Information Age,
mankind has made phenomenal progress.
Many secrets of Nature have been unearthed.
But there is almost no change in one respect.
As in the past, fear remains the main driving force.
Earlier, men were afraid of wild animals,
now they are afraid of one another.

****

One can overcome one's fears if one is prepared for the worst. But what is worst? It may turn out to be the best in the changed circumstances.

****

Just as the name of God is said
to be greater than God himself.
Similarly the fear of a calamity
is more harmful than the calamity itself.

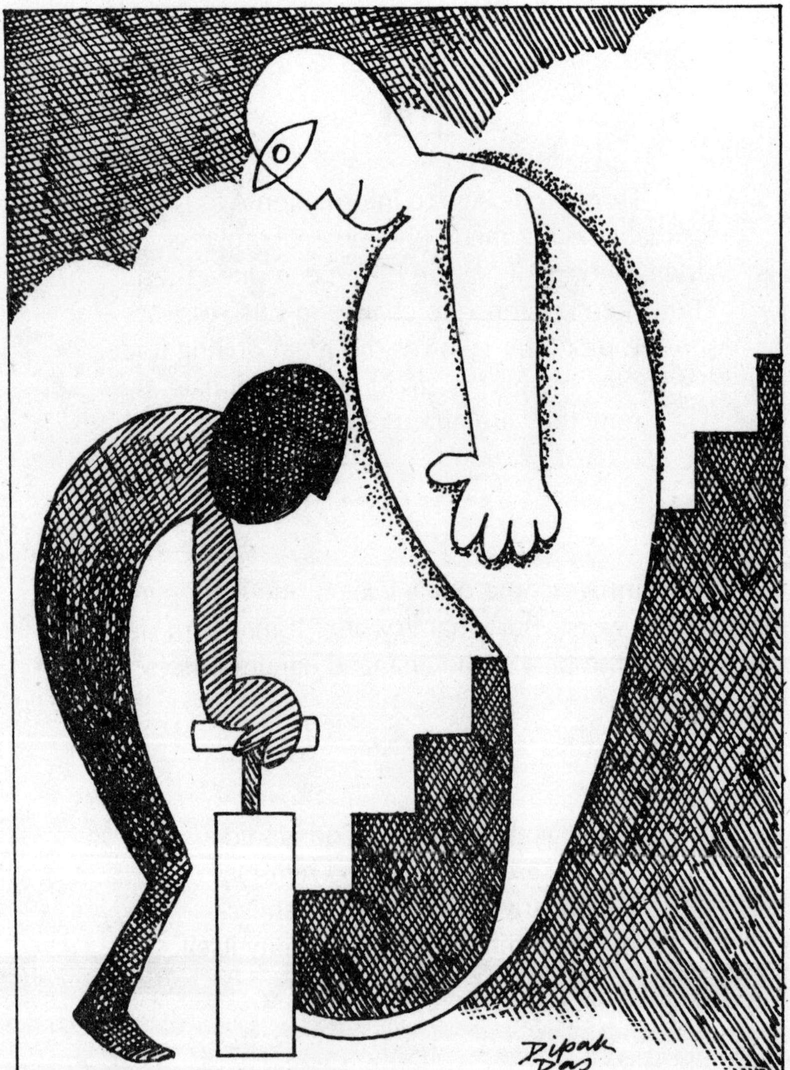
Dipak
Das

****

Fear was the root cause of all the wars fought in the history of mankind, either at the individual or at the collective level. Greed had only added fuel to the fire.

****

Do not let your heart be filled with fear. For in that case where would be the space left for love, affection and compassion.

Flattery

Do not flatter anyone undeservedly. When you do that, you stoop down in the same proportion as the other person is sought to be falsely lifted.

Friendship

If you consider someone a friend,
you may or may not actually make him one.
But if you consider him an enemy,
you are bound to make him one.

****

Nothing is permanent in this world.
An enemy may in fact be a friend
in the making.

****

Friendship is not based
on any idea of 'give' and 'take'.
It is a relationship wherein the processes of
giving and receiving merge into one.

Fundamentalism

Life is multi-faceted.
Fundamentalists are those
who are incapable of seeing
more than one facet of it.

G

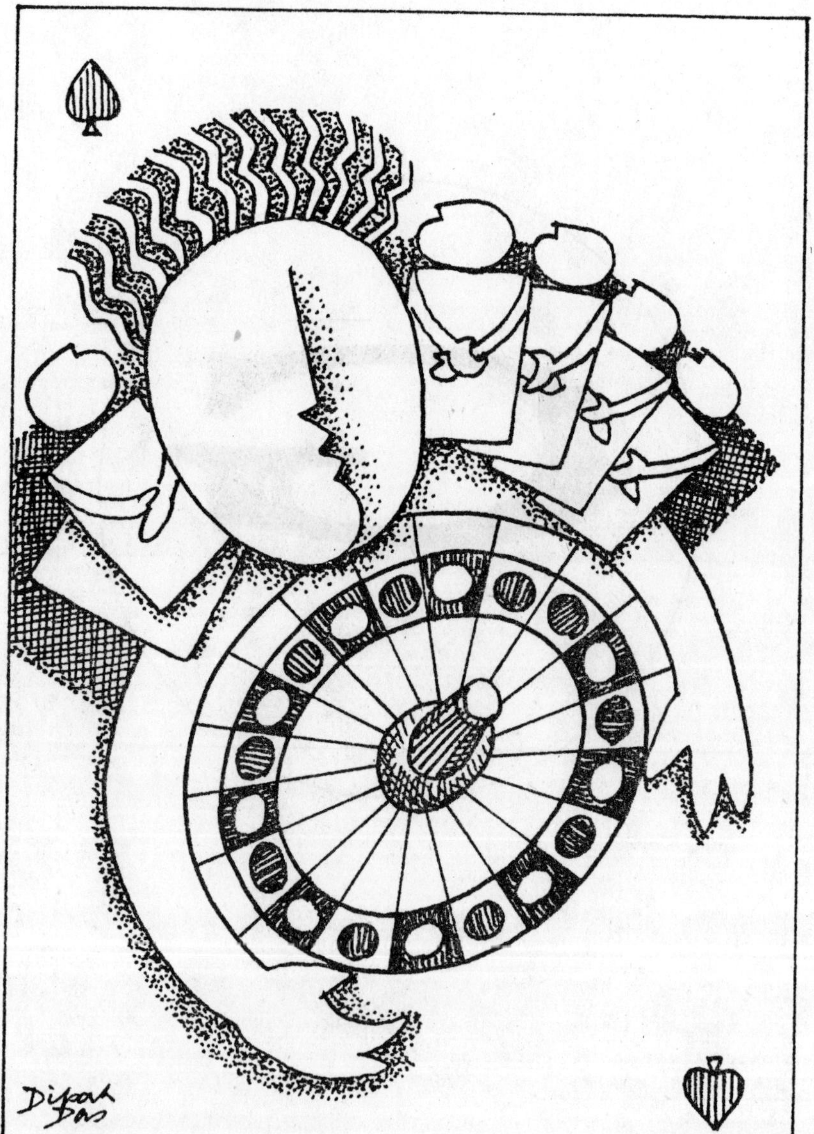

Gamble

Those who consider life as a gamble
are bound to lose, sooner than later.
And those who treat it as a struggle
are bound to win sooner or later.

Goals

An intelligent person explores
all means to achieve a goal.
A wise person, however, also examines
from time to time, the continued relevance of it.

****

Individuals may have different goals
depending on their will power,
nature and circumstances.
But the collective goal of mankind
shall continue to be the
health and happiness of all,
and complete harmony between everyone.
Every individual goal must be
in conformity with this universal goal.

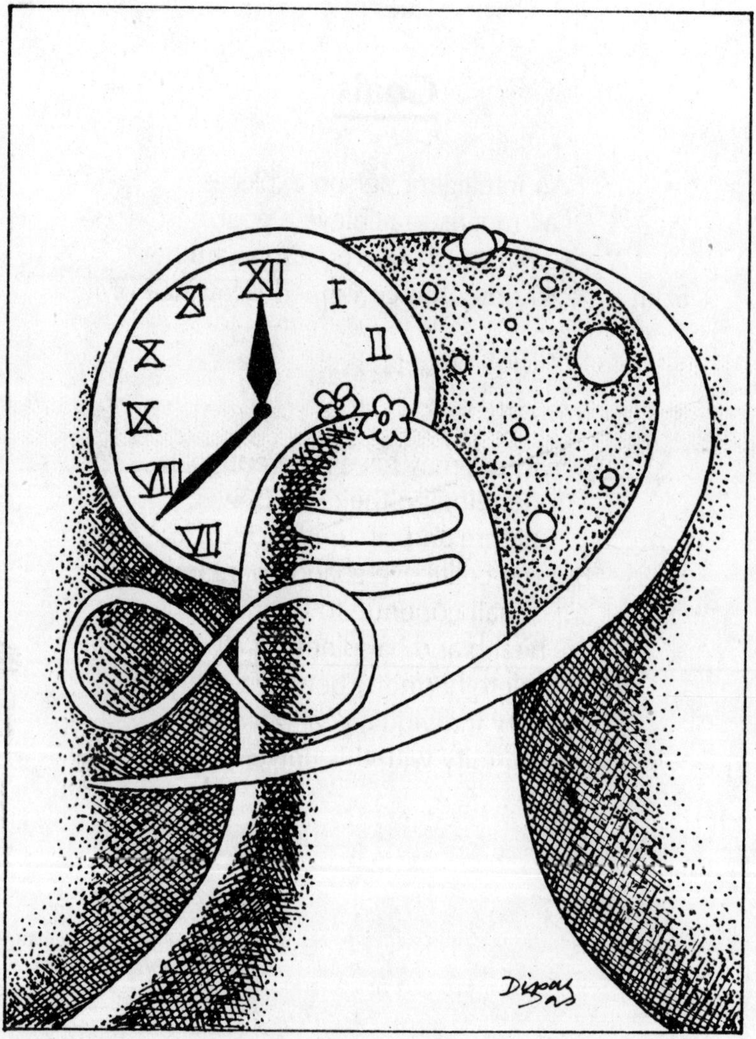

****

Well defined collective goal,
and individual freedom while working for that goal,
can bring the happiness of heaven
within the reach of every individual.

****

Calibre of individuals does not guarantee
the success of a group. What matters most is to
what extent they identify themselves with the
collective goals of the group.

God

Unwaivering faith in God,
and unfailing confidence in oneself,
are two aspects of the same mental condition.
The mental condition, that is,
of 'enhanced awareness'.

****

There can be nothing beyond God, as He is infinite.
Infinity plus or minus anything is infinity.
He is beyond the scope of limiting concepts
such as time and space.

****

Tie your string to the peg of Lord.
No harm can then come to you,
wherever you go and whatever you do.
For tied you would be to the strongest peg of them all.

****

No one other than God is perfect.
How perfect you shall be,
depends on how near you are to Him.

****

Those who worship idols, animals and plants are not necessarily polytheist. It is only symbolic of the fact that God is everywhere, including flora and fauna. He is, in fact, Omnipresent. He resides in objects inanimate, as well. Similarly, singers at graves do not necessarily worship the dead. They are only trying to search for the Divine element in the departed souls.

****

Never be God fearing.
Try, instead, to be God friendly.

Goodwill

To earn money is tough,
and it is tougher to earn goodwill.
But the latter can be expended
much faster than the former.

Guilt Feeling

One's enemies often try to condemn him for his actions of omission or commission. They may or may not succeed in their mission. But one's guilt feeling always succeeds in making one condemn oneself. Guilt feeling is one's worst enemy.

H

Health

Health is wealth, and much more. For whereas no amount of wealth can assure a good health, a healthy person can always earn a good living.

Heart

In biological terms, heart is a pump which purifies blood, metaphorically speaking, it is seat of the emotions. Let your heart be purified to the extent that even raw sentiments come out in the refined form.

History

History cannot be divided into eras based on some religious or other traditions. It is, in fact, a continuity of some recorded, and mostly unrecorded events experienced by mankind. Those events are like several light houses, which have guided and would continue to guide the mankind in its long journey in the sea of existence.

****

Some people tend to deny the existence of their own history prior to the happening of a particular event. Sympathize with them, for they are rootless people.

****

Stories of kings and queens represent only the cosmetic aspect of history. Real history should relate to the sufferings of common people, their aspirations and disappointments, and their successes and failures, from time to time.

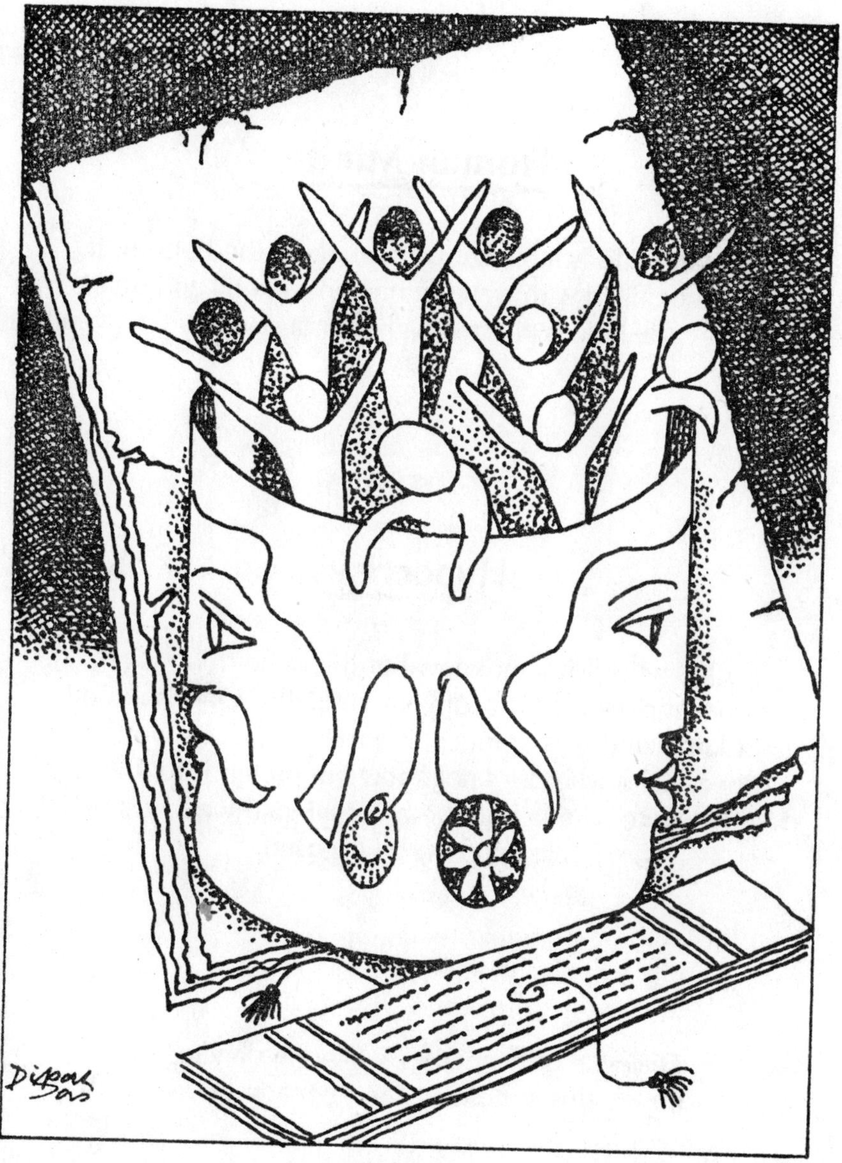
Dipak Das

Human Mind

Human mind is a bucket with a hole in the bottom. It cannot be filled with water of happiness untill and unless the hole is plugged with self-satisfaction.

Hypocrisy

One who does not know but thinks he does, is an innocent person worthy of your sympathy. One who does not know and says as much, is a truthful person worthy of respect. One who does not know but pretends to know, is a hypocrite who neither deserves sympathy nor respect. He needs to be exposed.

****

Dialogue of hypocrites is like the dancing of the shadows; nothing can be made out of it.

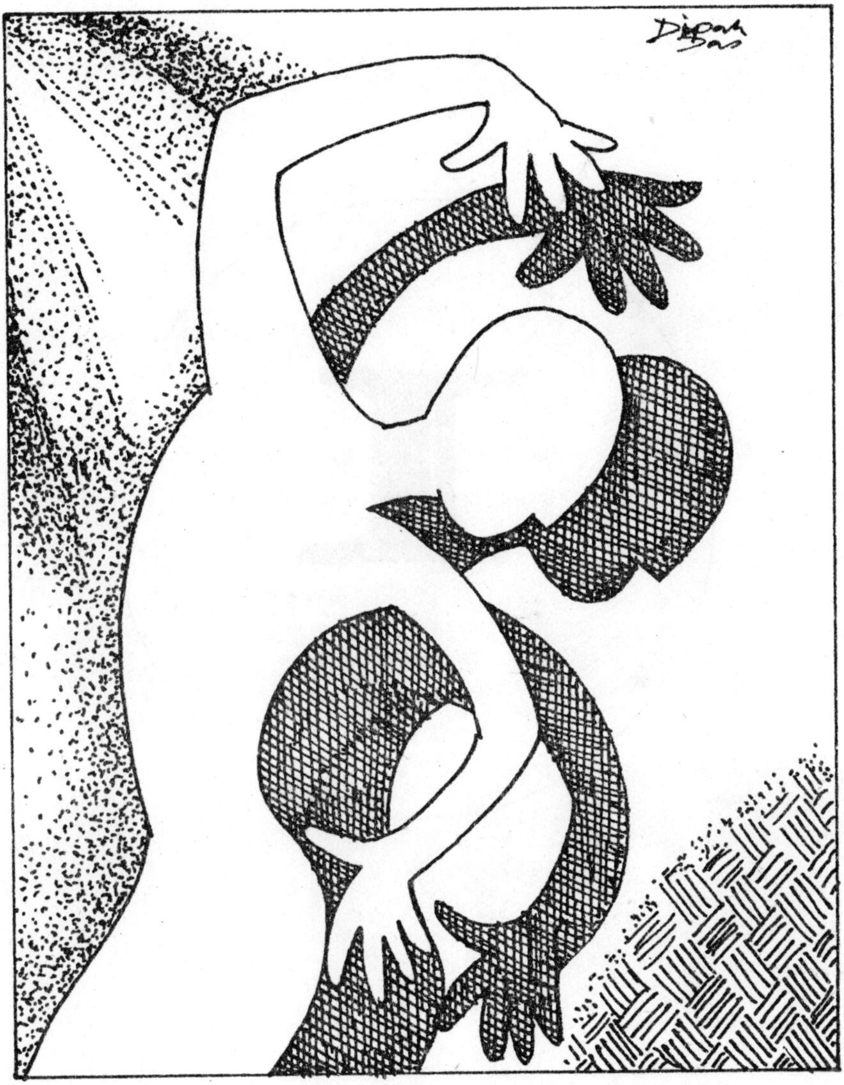
Dipak Das

Interaction

Everyone is capable of giving, and everyone also needs to receive which the others are capable of giving. The need is to create a platform where people can exchange ideas, and benefit from each other.

J

Dipak
Das

Jealousy

Thank the person who feels jealous of you.
He, at least, recognizes your superiority.

****

A jealous person is like a fried seed.
He cannot grow any further.

K

Kindness

The rich and the mighty
run the show of the world,
till they fall or are felled.
But only those who are kind
and considerate to others in
their hey day, can hope to
receive kindness in return, afterwards.

Knowledge

God is my guide as well. I asked Him to give me knowledge. He held my small finger and left me at the gate of the Garden of Knowledge. "Go as far into it as you can. Savour the flowers of knowledge and spread the message of their fragrance. But do not pluck them, for knowledge cannot be the exclusive right of any particular person or a particular group."

****

Thought process of man is limited
not by the lack of objects of knowledge
but by the limits of his own brain.

L

Last Laugh

Only those who can laugh at themselves,
can have the last laugh.

Law

One is simultaneously governed by two sets of rules, laws enacted by a particular society and laws of the Nature. Since laws of any society are an adaptation, howsoever imperfect, of divine laws, as understood by that society, more and more one functions in accordance with the universal code of conduct, there are lesser and lesser chances of his coming into conflict with the societal laws.

Leader

A leader is he who leads from the front;
and always keeps the rear in view.

****

A leader is he who calls nothing his own,
but for his people.

Learning

It is more important to learn the process of learning
than to acquire knowledge of different subjects,
because knowledge itself is a highly dynamic concept.

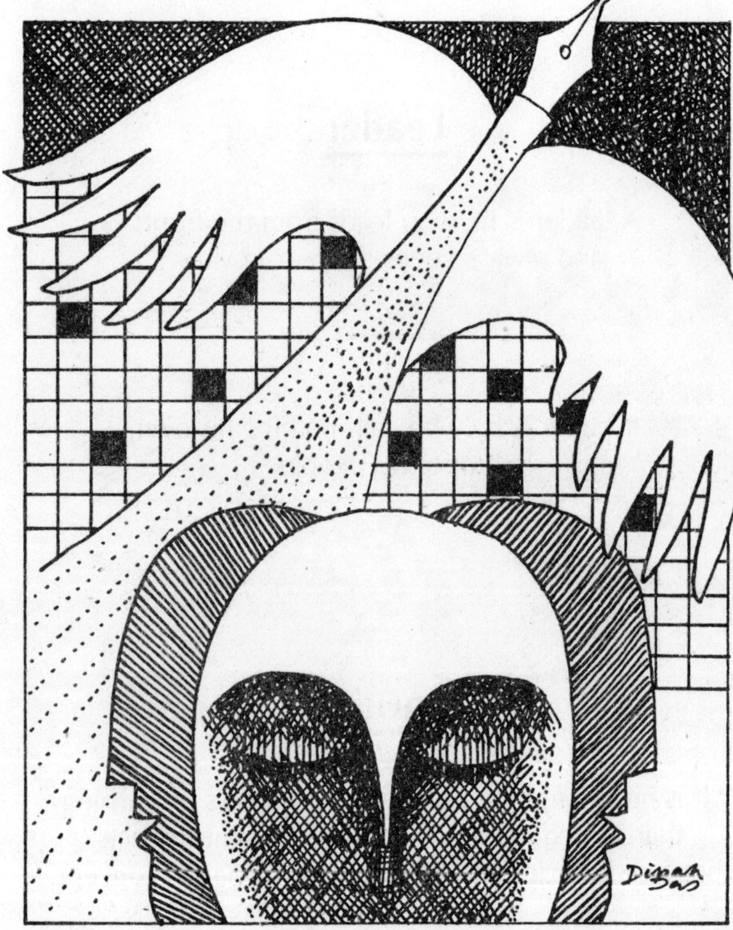

Life

If someone thinks that
he has understood the riddle of life,
he is probably looking at it
in a dangerously simplistic manner.

****

Life is a bundle of emotions
which present themselves
in different forms, shades and combinations
at any given point of time.

****

Life is a crossword puzzle
where one does not have to wait till it is solved.
The very process of solving brings rewards.

****

The concept of life after death is, in fact,
an infinite extension of survival instinct.

Dipak
Das

****

When there is so much to do in this life,
why bother about the next, if any.

****

Life can be seen as a hurdle's race. You have the option of participating in it or becoming a hurdle yourself.

****

Life is multi-faceted concept. Those who have been left behind in respect of any field i.e. physical, mental or spiritual, cannot claim to have won comprehensively the race of life.

****

Do not drag along life. Experience, instead, the joy of bumpy ride through lush green but thorny woods of life.

****

Life is not only a game of chance,
it is also a game of skill.

Limit

When the universe is so vast,
why limit yourself to the skies.

Living On The Edge

In the competitive world of today everyone is living on multiple border created by the dynamics of political, social, economic or other such forces. If one wants to live a secure life, he would have to learn to manage, if not resolve, as many borders as possible.

Logic

Succumb not to pressure,
and succumb not to pleasure.
Let the reason be your guide,
and logic your weapon.

****

Logic is the mother of all sciences.

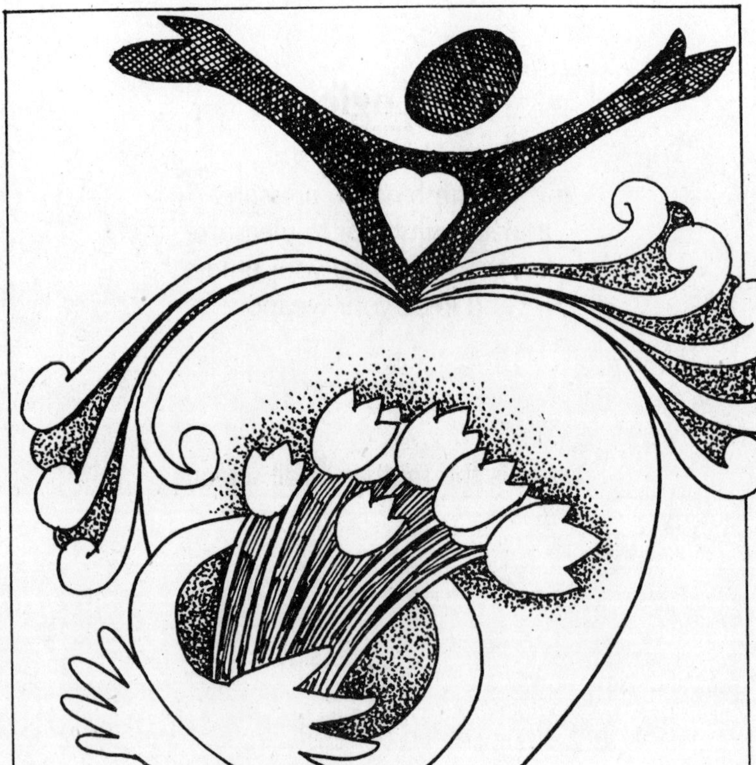

Love

Consider everyone worthy
of your faith, love and affection,
unless he proves himself to be unworthy of it.

****

Love is the glue that binds relationships.
All other emotions, including hate,
are only its variations.

Manager

Healthiest organ of your body is that of which you are least aware. Similarly, a good manager is one who is least visible. He is a facilitator and not an interventionist.

Marriage

Marriage, whether made in heaven or not,
can make life hell
if the lesson of mutual adjustment
is not well learnt.

Meditation

Meditation is the art of perceiving oneself apart from one's body and mind.

****

Object of meditation should not be to stop the thought process. It should rather be to control the mind and to harness its energy to achieve 'enhanced awareness'.

****

Some people think meditation is all about concentration. It is not. Purpose of meditation is to become aware of one's thoughts, acquire control over them, and to use them constructively. Concentration is only one of the means.

****

If ever you could record your thought process for a few seconds, it would go something like this. "The way Saddam has run away is really shameful. What bloddy Sharma thinks of........... Oh shit. This shoe is pinching. Amitabh was excellent in ?????. I have been humiliated. Let me do it today, from tomorrow no-way." Imagine the fate of the machine which is supposed to store and process such a disorganised data. Please remember, garbage in, garbage out. Obvious result is tension in mind and hypertension in body. If the rot is to be arrested the source would have to be cleansed.

****

Earlier, meditation was considered essential for those who were trying to find some deeper meaning to the phenomenon of life; but now it has become an absolute necessity for everyone, if any sanity is to be restored to the mad world of to-day.

Mistake

Mistake committed bona fide or otherwise,
has a natural tendency to multiply itself.
Therefore, it must be rectified
at the first available opportunity.

****

Till the time you realize your mistake,
you are bound to repeat it.

Money

Money is the lubricant of life.
Too little is ineffective,
whereas too much is a hindrance.

****

Money matters.
But the manner of its acquisition and utilization
matters even more.

N

Nature

Nature, can never be confined within any limiting concept. Those who define Nature in terms of some particular religious or philosophical principle, are either fooling themselves, or are trying to fool others.

****

When you merge yourself
with all your weaknesses with Nature,
you emerge stronger.

Neighbour

Know your neighbour. And also know yourself through his eyes.

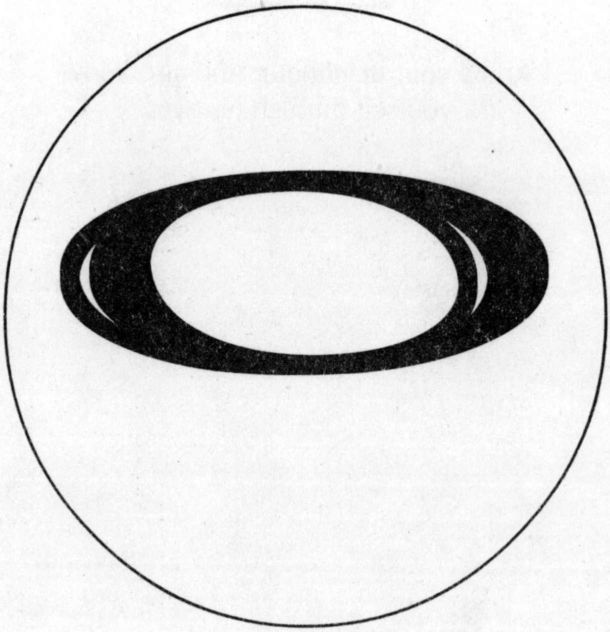

Opinion

A person who agrees with you always either has no opinion of his own or is not letting you know his real views. Either way, such a person cannot be depended upon.

X
IX
VIII
VII
III
IV
V

Opportunity

Any seemingly grim situation is an opportunity provided to you, by Nature, to prove your worth. If you can, you are a victor. If you cannot, you deserved only what you have got. Be satisfied with it.

****

Do not bother about the lost opportunity, for another is knocking at your door.

****

Opportunities rarely present themselves in their original form. They often appear in the form of challenges or problems.

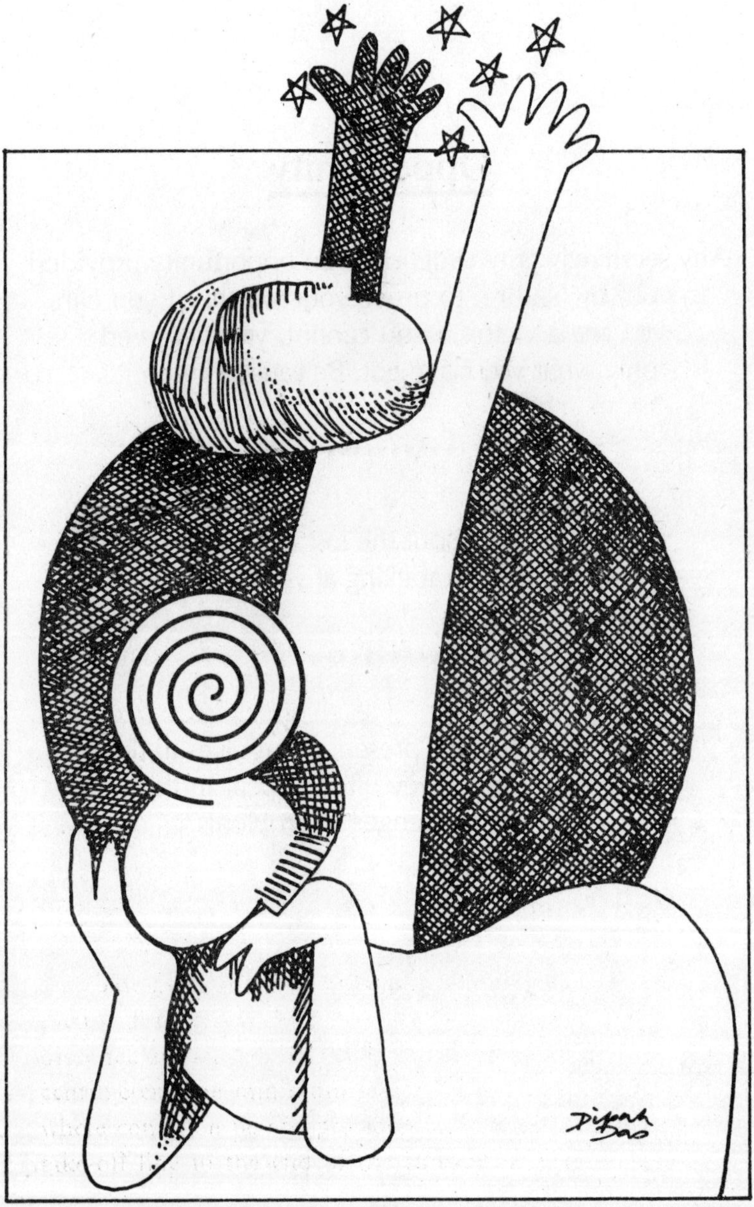

Optimist Vs. Pessimist

An optimist never looses hope, therefore, he utilises his energies at the optimum level. A pessimist concedes defeat even before the start of the race, therefore, he suffers the uncertainties of life passively.

P

Peace Of Mind

'Peace of mind' is a currency which can never be devalued. For the value of all other currencies is fixed with reference to that legal tender.

Playing Games

Those who are secretive in their dealings,
reveal only a part of their personality.
Surprisingly, they expect a part to achieve
what, according to them, the whole cannot.

****

Boasting is an expression
of dissatisfaction with oneself.
While boasting, one tries to fill the gap
between the reality and the desire, with falsehood.

Dipak Das

Potential

Everyone is born with a potential. To what extent one achieves that level depends upon (i) decisions taken (ii) efforts made and (iii) an unknown chance factor. Thus, two of the three ingredients of success are in one's own hands.

Power of Words

Appropriate, well meaning and sweet words can, sometimes, get results the like of which cannot be obtained by spending total wealth of whole of the world.

Prayer

Pray to God not for the things that are made by man, but for the qualities that make the man.

****

Prayer, when performed
with an attitude of total surrender,
functions as a great healer.

Problem

A problem which has no solution is yet to be created.

Progress

The Nature has not only hidden a secret in every atom of matter and every wave of energy, but has also provided mankind with wherewithal to unravel such mysteries. To explore such secrets and spread the resultant advantages over as wide a spectrum as possible, is what progress is all about. One of the criterion for writing report-card of successive generations is this.

Purpose of Life

If you think purpose of your life is enjoyment, enjoy to the maximum. If you think purpose of your life is making money, try to make as much money as no one has ever made. If you think purpose of your life is service to humanity, reach to the last person. If you think purpose of your life is to seek salvation, be free of all bondage, whatsoever. But you must have a clearly defined goal in life and put in all out efforts to achieve the same.

R

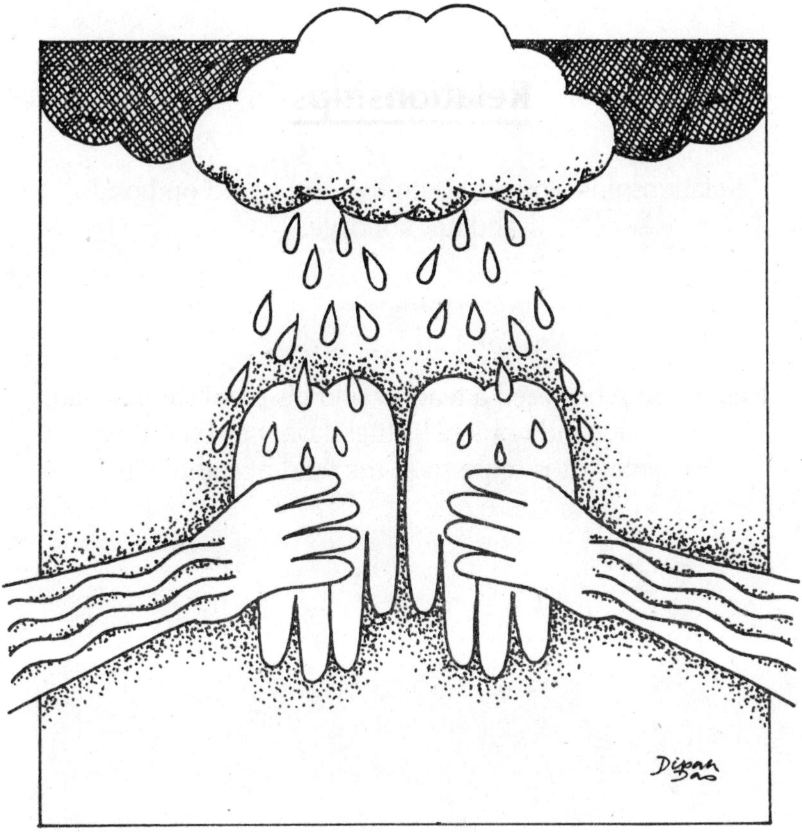
Dipak Das

Relationships

Relationships blossom when they are based on bonds, and not bondage.

****

Relationship between a teacher and his pupil should lead to learning and not intellectual slavery or emotional blackmail. It is more so in the field of spirituality.

Religion

Formal religion is often like an opaque wall
through which no outside view is possible.
Even when it does let in some light,
it is too diffused to see anything.
Liberal, open and transparent religion
is the need of the hour.

****

Ancient faiths which cannot stand the test
of accepted scientific findings,
need to re-examine themselves
and re-assess their tenets.
That is what is maturing with time.

****

Those religions which do not admit of any path of salvation, other than their own, are more oppressive in nature. They are excessively protective as they run the risk of being exposed in an atmosphere of openness.

Reputation

Before doing or deciding not to do something, please remember that in addition to your own self you represent a family, a community, a generation and much more. So many reputations are simultaneously at stake.

Results of Actions

Perpetrator of a crime may or may not be punished by courts of law. But under no circumstances can anyone ever escape the psychological and spiritual consequences of one's actions. Every action is invariably accompanied by sometimes visible but mostly invisible consequences which is its own instantaneous, automatic and self-contained punishment or reward, as the case may be.

Revenge

Revenge is the cost one wants to inflict on someone for the damage perceived to have been caused to oneself by that person. At the same time, it is the justification he provides to that person for inflicting further damage on him.

Dipak
Das

Right

Might may or may not always be right.
But right always has its own might.

Ripple Effect

Every action performed, relationship established or feeling expressed not only affects the persons concerned but also has an infinite ripple effect. Therefore, caution is of utmost importance, before indulging in any of the above activities.

S

Self-confidence

Droplets of individual egos, which constantly suffer from feeling of insecurity can, by mutual caring and sharing, merge themselves to form a huge sea where nothing else but self-confidence would flow.

****

Those who are confident that they can, can. And those who are afraid that they cannot, cannot.

Dipak Das

Self Realisation

Law of diminishing returns
does not apply to the joy
generated out of self-realisation.

Sharing

Stoop to learn, toil to earn. And to get maximum out of the two share them with others.

Skewed Priority

Man has so far not been able
to provide decent life to all its tribe.
He has, however, succeeded
in equipping himself with weapons
which can destroy the mankind many
times over. Are his priorities right?

Smile

Even a forced smile is capable of not only
neutralising bad feelings but also creating
a feel good factor. Imagine the avalanche
of healthy emotions a genuine smile can generate.

Sorrow Versus Happiness

At any given point of time,
two types of forces are knocking at one's door;
those that lead to sorrow,
and those that lead to happiness.
Sometimes, knocking by the forces
of darkness may be louder.
Whom to let in and whom not to,
that decision is always of the person concerned.

Spirituality

Spirituality is the balm, as it were,
that sooths the nerves of mankind,
frayed by millions of years of conflicts
in the name of race, religion, and sovereignty etc.

****

Whereas spirituality refers to the
natural urge of man to know his Creator,
religion is the self-proclaimed agent which claims
to have the wherewithal to get that urge satisfied.

****

Spiritualism is the substance of
inquiry into the purpose of life.
Religious groups, sects and philosophies
represent various forms of that inquiry.

****

There is no inherent conflict between
progress and prosperity on the one hand,
and moral values and spirituality on the other.
In fact, they supplement each other.

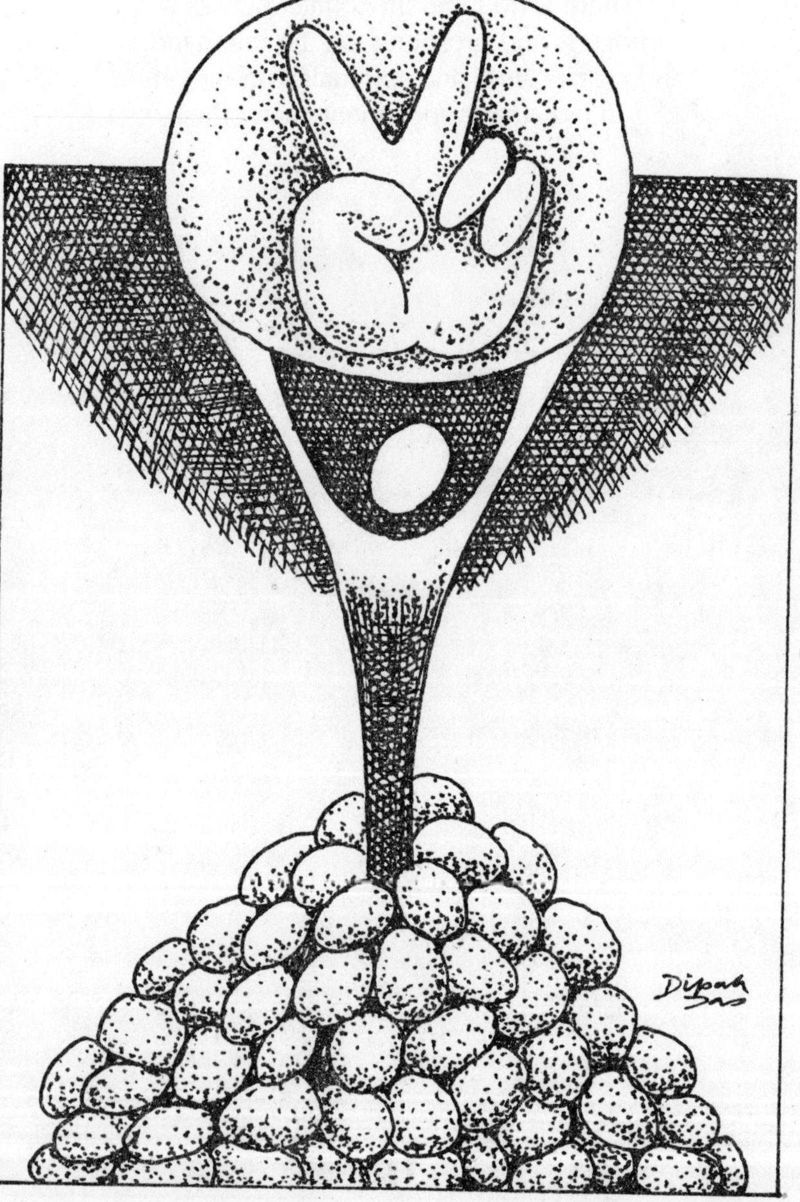

Success

Road to success often emerges
out of small pathways of hard labour.

****

There can be no universal scale to measure success.
One parameter can be how much one has achieved
with reference to one's circumstances.
The other must be how.

Suffering

Very few sufferings on anyone are inflicted by an
act of God or an act of omission or commission of
someone else. Source of miseries lies mainly in oneself.
Solution lies where the problem does.

Suicide

There is only one crime against humanity which is worse than murder, for it goes against the most fundamental principle of self-preservation. That is suicide. Most unfortunate part is that it goes unpunished in the court of man.

Superstition

Never bother what a superstitious person does for he is not an agent of his own free will.

Surface Tension

Law of physics tells us that there is tension at the surface. To experience real peace, let us delve deep into whatever we do.

Surrender

Surrender to the Lord costs you nothing. It is a trade in which net profit is equal to the gross revenue.

Sycophant

A sycophant is your worst enemy
because he does not let you know the truth.
And when the reality explodes in your face,
he is nowhere to be seen.

****

A sycophant puts patches
of flattery on your torn ego.
If you have no holes in your personality,
why let sycophants come near you.

T

Teaching

Teaching is not only about transfer of knowledge.
It is also about sharing of knowledge.

Terrorism

Only those who are terrorised from within
try to spread terrorism outside.

The Present Moment

One need not strive to be a person
of a century, a decade or a year.
Be a person of the moment.
Take the present moment in firm grip.
Years, decades or centuries are bound to follow.

****

Every moment is pregnant with opportunity.
Let it be delivered to the right person,
at the right place, and in the right manner.

****

Only link between the past and the future
is the present. Both have relevance only
with reference to the present.

****

Just three moments determine one's life.
Moment of one's birth,
moment of one's death and
the present moment.
One has no control of the first.
Control of the second is also
very little. Let the third be used in
the most constructive manner.

Theocracy

A theocratic state is a dark room where all windows of knowledge, except one, are sought to be shut forever.

Time

Some people say time is money. Importance of time should never be belittled to this extent.

Tradition

Do not follow a bad tradition.
For in that case you are not only responsible
for your own action, but are also burdened
with the consequences of actions of others.

Truth Versus Falsehood

The truth is description of facts as they are. Falsehood, on the other hand, is represented by the masks with which such facts are sought to be concealed. Any truth does not need the services of an outside agency to prove itself. Truth can neither be created nor destroyed by anyone. Falsehood, on the other hand, is not only created by vested interests but also needs their constant support to survive. Truth is perpetual whereas the falsehood survives only till the time truth is hidden. Thus, by its very definition, falsehood is least dependable. Rely upon it only when it is absolutely essential.

Uncertainties Of Life

Beauty of life lies in its uncertainties. A person whose demise is predicted with precision, is condemned to a pre-mature and painful death.

W

War

Wage a war against weaknesses and evils of your own, of your community, of the society at large. Others would take care of themselves.

****

Wage a war not only for your right,
but also for what is right.

Wealth

Generation of wealth is the legitimate right
and even the social duty of a person.
But degeneration of the individual,
in the process, is an unacceptable cost.

****

Wealth, like technology, is a good servant,
but a very bad master.

Will Power

Will power is the capacity of a person to make his mind as well as his body carry out his rational decisions.

****

Human mind, like body, is ever evolving. Will-power of the individual concerned is an important input which influences in a big way the result of this evolutionary process.

Witness

You are witness to your own deeds,
more than anyone else can ever be.
Never ever be hostile to your own witness,
never ever be untrue to your own self.

Work

Just as motion keeps a machine from rusting,
So also work and challenge keep a man
from falling into sloth.

****

Work delayed is work multiplied by a factor,
which is directly proportional to the period of
delay. The incremental work is always
unproductive work.

****

Dreams are gaseous, and can take one anywhere. Planning is liquid, and has its limitations. But it is only hard work which can give a solid shape to one's ambitions.

****

A balance between physical and mental work is needed to keep the mind and body in good health. Industrialisation and automation have disturbed this balance. Health of man would continue to suffer till the balance is restored.

****

Man can be defined in terms of body, mind and awareness. However, a more appropriate method of defining an individual could be the work assigned to him and the quality of his performance.

****

Only those who know how to enjoy the work assigned to them can ever hope to realise the real meaning of enjoyment.

Dipak Das

Worry

Do not worry about your work;
work, instead, on your worries.

****

'Do worry, and be unhappy'.
A great majority would not approve of this slogan.
Nonetheless, they follow it most religiously.

Worship

Those who worship Him sincerely and without any expectation, need not ask Him for anything; as He realises their genuine needs, much before the same are felt by them.

****

God, though formless Himself, can be realized in whatever form He is worshipped.

Dipak Das

Younger Generation

It is not desirable to describe younger generation as better or worse for it cannot be measured with the yardstick of others. If they do not adhere to any value system, elders are to be blamed, in one way or the other. They could neither instill their values in them; nor did they enable them to develop their own.

Z

Zeal Of Life

Every child has a dream to change whole of the world, where as a man in the evening of his life does not even think of changing his own style. Age, thus, should be measured not by years but by the zeal for life, which in turn depends upon capacity to dream.